the
Designer
Originals

the Designer Originals

WOMEN WHOM GOD CREATED TO STAND ON THE FRONT LINE OF TIME IN MINISTRY

Dr. Mary Smith-McCoy

iUniverse, Inc.
Bloomington

THE DESIGNER ORIGINALS
WOMEN WHOM GOD CREATED TO STAND ON
THE FRONT LINE OF TIME IN MINISTRY

iUniverse books may be ordered through booksellers or by contacting:

iUniverse
1663 Liberty Drive
Bloomington, IN 47403
www.iuniverse.com
1-800-Authors (1-800-288-4677)

Because of the dynamic nature of the Internet, any web addresses or links contained in this book may have changed since publication and may no longer be valid. The views expressed in this work are solely those of the author and do not necessarily reflect the views of the publisher, and the publisher hereby disclaims any responsibility for them.

Any people depicted in stock imagery provided by Thinkstock are models, and such images are being used for illustrative purposes only.
Certain stock imagery © Thinkstock.

ISBN: 978-1-4759-9350-9 (sc)
ISBN: 978-1-4759-9351-6 (ebk)

Library of Congress Control Number: 2013909849

Printed in the United States of America

iUniverse rev. date: 06/11/2013

Table of Contents

Introduction

There are women that God has called and anointed to preach the gospel of Jesus Christ.

They have been awakened to make a difference in the world in which we live. They refuse to be individuals that are blending in with those who have chosen to be by-standers, on—lookers, and those who have refused to allow God to use them. In this book you will find women who are brave and who walk in victory. They are women who refuse to be silent and cowards in their walk with Christ. Yes, they are women who will walk in the fruit of the spirit and call sin, sin. They are women in Christ who will not settle for things of this life; that will not bring glory to God, due to the commitment to take a stand for Jesus Christ. It is time for women everywhere to rise up and take their God given place in the body of Christ. As women we have remained behind the curtain of time for far too long. We have not allowed God to use us for such a time as this.

There are women that God has anointed and called to ministry, "cry aloud, spare not, lift up thy voice like a trumpet, and show my people their transgressions, and the house of Jacob for their sins." (Isaiah 58:1) People like Apostle Dr. Mary Austin Jones, Apostle Dr. Jeannette C. Holmes-Vann, Bishop Dr. Carolyn Boston Love and other women who are not ashamed of the gospel of Christ, "for they know that it is the power of God unto salvation to every one that believeth; to the Jew first and also to the Greek." (Romans 1:16)

Yes, these women are of every color, culture, and many of them are standing in a place of obedience. They are going forth to make the devil back up and back out of the lives of God's people. They are carrying the light of Jesus into their families, jobs, businesses, and where ever they can make a difference. They are in every city in the United States of America, many are on foreign soil. They do not care how far their mission will take them because they are on assignment for Christ.

When we think of these women of God: Apostle Dr. Mary Austin Jones, Apostle Dr. Jeannette C. Holmes-Vann, and Bishop Dr. Carolyn Boston Love we can see how God will use His people to do great and mighty things. He will position them in places of influence, to advance His kingdom, and to save those who are captive. In the bible, just as God called Esther into the kingdom for such a time as this (Esther 4:14). God had allowed circumstances to happen in their lives, in preparation for what He wanted to do on behalf of His people. God is looking for bold and courageous women in our government. He wants those who will stand for what's right and righteousness. He wants those who will represent Him in the White House as well as your house, in congress, in the senate, as well as in any public place, so that He can be glorified and praised. Women of God it is your time to rise and shine, to show the world how God wants His people to represent Him; our loving God and Father who has been faithful and righteous to all of us.

It does not matter how trying our situations are in life, God always make a way of escape for those who trust and believe in His word. Get ready as the Designer Originals introduce to you more women whom God has ordained to receive Provision, Access, and Favor. Women God created to stand on the front line of time in Ministry.

Dedication

I dedicate my first book, *The Designer Originals*, to Jesus Christ, my heavenly Father, to my parents, the late Mr. Arthur and Mrs. Fannie Mae Smith, to my husband and Father of our children, Mr. Larry McCoy. He has supported me in ministry since the day we were married. Also, I dedicate this book to my two children, my beautiful daughter, Stephanie Dionne McCoy Boykins and my handsome son, Patrick Douglas McCoy.

I am blessed with two wonderful sisters, Dr. Petty Jean Smith Pender and retired Master Sergeant Cynthia Smith. To my brothers Mc Arthur Smith, Anthony Smith and Wesley Smith (Deceased 9/2009) I Love you very much. I would also like to thank my extended family all whose names I am unable to mention, please know I Love and thank God for each of you. I dedicate the Designer Original to my cousin Bishop Robert Lee Jones and to my beautiful Goddaughter Tanedra Cardona-Dance.

Dr. Mary Smith—McCoy

We live in a day in which God is taking women to a place in ministry that has been hidden under the scope of time. Women have not always been accepted as laborious in ministry, as preacher and teacher of the Gospel of Jesus Christ.

Women have been called to bring the light of Jesus into dark places, to give men and women a view, and vision of God in His greatness.

Eve the Designer's Original

When God made the woman, He had Adam in mind. I believe that Adam appreciated the fact that God gave him a woman by his side; He was blessed to enjoy the awesome things God himself created in the garden and on Earth. She was a Designer Original, created to share in the life of the man called Adam.

The Creation of Eve

Genesis 2:21-25

And the Lord God caused a deep sleep to fall upon Adam, and he slept: and He took one of his ribs, and closed up the flesh instead thereof;

And the rib, which the Lord God had taken from man, made He a woman, and brought her to the man.

And Adam said, This is now bone of my bones, and flesh of my flesh: she shall be called Woman, because she was taken out of Man.

Therefore shall a man leave his father and his mother, and shall cling to his wife: and they shall be one flesh.

And they were both naked, the man and his wife, and were not ashamed.

Genesis 3: 1-24

Now the serpent was more subtle than any beast of the field which the Lord God had made. And he said to the woman, Yea, has God said, You shall not eat of every tree of the garden?

And the woman said to the serpent, We may eat of the fruit of the trees of the garden:

But of the fruit of the tree which is in the midst of the garden, God has said, You shall not eat of it, neither shall you touch it, less you die.

And the serpent said to the woman, You shall not surely die.

For God does know that in the day you eat thereof, then your eyes shall be opened, and you shall be as god, knowing good and evil.

And when the woman saw that the tree was good for food, and a tree to be desired to make one wise, she took of the fruit thereof, and did eat and gave also to her husband with her; and he did eat.

And the eyes of them both were opened, and they knew that they were naked: and they sewed fig leaves together, and made themselves aprons.

And they heard the voice of the Lord God walking in the garden in the cool of the day: and Adam and his wife hid themselves from the presence of the Lord God among the trees of the garden.

And the Lord God called to Adam, and said to him, Where are you?

And he said, I heard your voice in the garden, and I was afraid, because I was naked; and I hid myself.

And He said, who told you that you were naked? Have you eaten of the tree, whereof I commanded you that you should not eat?

And the man said, The woman whom You gave to be with me, she gave me of the tree, and I did eat.

And the Lord God said to the woman, what is this that you have done? And the woman said, The serpent beguiled me, and I did eat.

And the Lord God said to the serpent, Because you have done this, you are cursed above all cattle, and above every beast of the field; upon your belly shall you go, and dust shall you eat all the days of your life:

And I will put enmity between you and the woman, and between your seed and her seed: it shall bruise your head, and you shall bruise his heel.

To the woman He said, I will greatly multiply your sorrows you shall be to your husband, and he shall rule over you.

And to Adam He said, Because you have hearkened to the voice of your wife, and have eaten of the tree, of which I commanded you, saying, You shall not eat of it: cursed is the ground for your sake; in sorrow shall you eat of it all the days of your life;

Thorns also and thistle shall it bring forth to you; and you shall eat the herbs of the field;

In the sweat of your face shall you eat bread, till you return to the ground; for out of it were you taken: for dust you are, and to dust shall you return.

And Adam called his wife name Eve; because she was the mother of all living.

To Adam also and to his wife did the Lord God make coats of skin, and clothed them.

And the Lord God said, Behold, the man is become as one of Us, to know good and evil: and now, less he put forth his hand, and take also of the tree of life, and eat, and live for ever:

Therefore the Lord God sent him forth from the garden of Eden, to till the ground from where he was taken.

So He drove out the man; and He placed at the east of the garden of Eden Cherubims, and a flaming sword which turned every way, to keep the way of the tree of life.

Disobedient and Unfaithful

Women have always been curious about their surroundings. They are bound to question things they do not understand. This may not always be the right thing to do? As we shall see, Eve was in the garden and she allowed the serpent to use her to eat the fruit that God had instructed them not to eat from the one tree in garden. Eve was disobedient and unfaithful to the God who created her. She convinced Adam to go against God's instructions. Both of them had to pay the awful price of leaving the Garden of Eden.

God saw fit to give them a chance to live and provide for themselves and for their family by working for everything they needed.

As women, we may appear to be the weaker vessel in physical strength. In contrast, with that thought we have the strength to be there for our husbands and children; to teach and love them. We have the strength to multi-task in various ways; something that seems impossible for the average man.

The woman of God did not make this a time of defeat, but a time that she and her husband were able to use to be fruitful and to multiply and replenish Earth.

When Did Women's Ministry Begin?

Women were first called to love the God that made and created them. They were called to love their husbands, to love, and care for their children.

Some women begin their ministry when they are good wives to the men that God has given them. They begin their ministry when they begin to be great teachers to their children and to the people God has placed in their lives.

If you were to ask me if women are perfect, I would say, "They are not." They are called for such a time as this; to save and rescue the lives of the people around them. They have been called to help those who are far off course and to keep them away from the pits of Hell.

Reaching the Lost for Christ

Women of God have been called to reach the lost at any cost. We cannot deny this call on our lives. God has placed something inside of women that has made them curious, unafraid to go forth, conquer all that seems to be impossible.

We are women on the front line. We are not afraid to go into the hedges and highways; to compel men, women, boys and girls to be saved, and to give their lives to Almighty God.

Yes, we are all different and God made us different for many reasons. He did this because we are able and willing to go forth and make a difference in this lifetime.

Women on the Front Line

There are women who are standing on the front lines each day of their lives, who are not afraid to go into battle for souls to be saved. These women know that God has not given them the spirit of fear but of love, power and a sound mind. (2 Timothy 1:7) There are women everywhere, in all walks of life. The question I have is have all of them been given the same assignment?

No! Some are apostles, prophets, evangelists, pastors, and teachers that are in the body of Christ.

Jesus Christ has commissioned all of us to go into the hedges and highways, to compel men, women, boys, and girls to be saved.

As people of God, we are all called.

We are called to be fishers of men and ambassadors for Christ. Regardless of our title or the marketplace we minister. We can all win souls for the kingdom of God.

Apostle Dr. Mary Austin Jones Woman of Faith Power and the Anointing

Apostle Mary Austin Jones, Founder of the *We're for Jesus House of Prayer*, was a trailblazer and a woman who was used greatly by the Almighty God.

She was a woman who dared to be different. She was willing to challenge others to rise to the call of God in their lives.

She was a visionary who took God at His word. She was one who decided to follow Jesus and to walk in the supernatural to do great and mighty things for her God. She had faith to heal the sick and to raise the dead.

She defies the unbeliever who chooses not to take God at His Word. Apostle Dr. Mary Austin Jones was born to Mr. Charlie and Deloris Austin on February 17, 1947. She was educated in the Duval County school system and lived a life as an honor student, and role model in her youth.

She did not come from a well-known family, and she was not wealthy in her earlier life. As a child, she often went to school with shoes that were too big for her feet. She knew that there was something on the inside that was calling her to her father's business.

She was married to Apostle Robert Lee Jones, who departed this life on May 18, 2012. He was so loved by many. He was called by God to put water on the dry bone and to preach to those who needed life through the word of God. They were blessed with the births of Toris, Tawanna, and Isreal Jones, each of who now works in ministry.

Apostle Dr. Mary Austin Jones chose to obey the word of God on April 30, 1976. She accepted Jesus Christ as her personal Lord and Savior; a Born-Again, Holy Ghost-filled believer. She immediately began to witness; tell others about Jesus Christ, and His Goodness.

Special Encounter with God

She had a special encounter with God just as Paul did on the road to Damascus. There he met the Lord. In this way, God showed her purpose. He desired her to fulfill that purpose.

Apostle Jones was called and chosen to deliver those who were bound, held captive and imprisoned by invisible walls. She was called to heal the broken-hearted and to bind up their wounds. She was called to preach the word in and out of season.

Demonstration of God's Power

She started out in her home, teaching and preaching the word of God. She later converted their garage into a chapel, where she led a life-changing and fire-baptizing service every Saturday. This is where the fire of the God Spirit entered and many souls were saved. Lives were renewed through the preaching and demonstration of the power of the most High God.

There were many that came and who filled every seat to capacity in her small chapel. They came with excitement and expectation as they looked toward God to show up and show out. Bodies were healed, demons were cast out, and much deliverance was manifested through the word of God.

Miracle after Being Given Six Months to Live

In 1980, a young lady named Sarah was rushed to the hospital with severe pain in her lower abdomen.

After the examination, her mother was called aside by doctors who informed her that Sarah needed emergency exploratory surgery.

During the surgery, the doctors found that Sarah had fourteen cancerous tumors; as well as pancreatitis, appendicitis, and a gallstone.

The doctors were amazed that this young woman had so many health problems. After surgery, she continued to go in and out of the hospital in order to recover. She spent almost an entire year in the hospital.

Sarah had a friend who knew Christ and invited Sarah to go to church with her. Together they attended a noon-day service; on September 15[th.] She remembered the day well because she was again scheduled to have surgery. Sarah was tired of being cut into and poked by the doctors. She was ready to try something else.

After the Pastor finished preaching, she was the very first person called out. She stood and the Pastor said, "God had a healing for her."

Supernatural Healing by God

Pastor Mary Austin Jones rested her anointed hands on Sarah, who remembers falling to the floor at once. When she got up she knew that something had changed. The doctors had given her six months to live at the time. Now it is more than thirty years later and Sarah is yet alive. She is still praising and thanking God for taking the strips on His back, so that she would not have to die. Never again would she have to be sick.

In that service, God miraculously healed her body. When I think of the mission of the twelve disciples in the book of Matthew 10:5-8, from the King James Version, it reads:

These twelve Jesus sent forth, and commanded them, saying, 'Go not into the way of the Gentile, and into any city of the Samaritan enter ye not. But go rather to the lost sheep of the house of Israel. And as ye go, preach, saying the kingdom of heaven is at hand. Heal the sick, cleanse the lepers, and raise the dead, cast out devils: freely ye have received, freely give. Matthew 10:5-8

Man Raised from the Dead

This woman of God was used to raise the dead. A man was sick, the doctors pronounced him dead, and the doctors left out of the room. Apostle Mary Austin Jones did not use more of the same methods the doctors used, such as more medication, or the defibrillator or more C.P.R.

Instead she prayed over this man with the faith that she had in Jesus Christ. God restored life back into his body.

Lazarus Raise from the Dead

That act reminding me of Jesus when He raised Lazarus from the dead in the Gospel of St. John the 11th chapter, when the unbelievers thought it was all over for Lazarus. There was no longer breath in his body, the blood was not circulating through his veins, he could no longer see, feel, move, speak, or hear. They prepared his body and put him away, bound with grave clothes. What they did not realize was that it was not over until God said it was over.

The scripture tells us that Jesus came to see Mary and Martha after Lazarus had been dead for four days. Jesus Christ asked them to show Him where they had laid him.

Jesus said, "Take ye away the stone." Martha, the sister of he who was dead saith unto him, "Lord, by this time he stinketh: for he hath been dead four days."

Jesus saith unto her, "Said I not unto thee, that if thou wouldest believe, thou shouldest see the glory of God?"

Then they took away the stone from the place where the dead had been laid. And Jesus lifted up his eyes, and said, "Father, I thank thee that thou hast heard me. I knew that thou hearest me always the people which standby I said it, that they may believe that thou hast sent me."

When he thus had spoken, he cried with a loud voice and Lazarus came forth. He that was dead came forth, bound hand and foot with graveclothes. His face was bound about with a napkin. Jesus saith unto them, "Loose him, and let him go." (John 11:17-44)

I do not remember how many years this man lived afterward, but Dr. Mary Austin Jones performed the miracle of faith saying that, "God used her to speak life into his body by the power of the Almighty God; in the name of Jesus." I do know that God is a miracle-working God. He who was dead was brought back to life.

Barren Woman Receive A Miracle

There was another young woman who wanted children along with her husband. The woman suffered from endometriosis and was barren. Apostle Mary Austin Jones prayed for her by faith in the Almighty God. She and her husband were able to have not one, but three daughters during their marriage.

The word of God says to ask, and it shall be given you; seek and you shall find; knock, and it shall be opened to you. What are you waiting for? Ask and believe and you shall receive.

God Will Provide

The faith of this woman of God, she did not take an offering for a long time. She decided to trust God and let God supply the needs of the ministry. This trailblazer gave her own substance in order to minister to the needs of God's people.

I believe that she only wanted to do the will of the father. She wanted to do what others only talked about doing, but did not have the faith to believe God to walk in the anointing of the Almighty God.

When the people came in Saturday, the chapel was so full that, the people had to stand on the outside to hear, the woman of God preach the word of God.

Apostle Dr. Mary Jones lived in Jacksonville, Florida, in a community called Sherwood Forest. At that time her husband, Dr. Robert Lee Jones, worked as a police officer for the city of Jacksonville. He was very faithful to God and to Apostle Mary Austin Jones. Every Saturday, he and their children would help the woman of God prepare for service. It did not matter about the shift that he worked. She could always depend on him to help her in ministry.

As time went on the size of the congregation that came each Saturday grew. The woman of God began to seek the face of God and they purchased their first church on the Westside of town. The church was called *"We're For Jesus House of Prayer Westside."* It began with only forty adults and sixty children when they purchased the church.

God did the Miraculous with only a few people, so that He would receive the glory, honor, and the praise.

Faith Moves God

The first church was purchased and completely paid off in five months! The church was paid off using only tithes and offerings!

There were no car washes, no selling of fried chicken, no fish fries, cake bakes or any of these things. Instead, it was her trust in our God, and the obedience to His Word.

Due to her obedience to God, He moved in the supernatural and filled this church too. There were extra chairs that had to be set out for the people, so that they too could hear the word of God.

Can you believe that even with the size of our new church building, people were still sitting outside to hear the word of God? Yes, our God is a miracle-working God.

Dr. Mary Austin Jones continued to move in signs and wonder by the hand of God. There were people who came from around the city to hear this anointed woman of God. Souls were saved and lives were forever changed.

God continued to show up in a remarkable and awesome way. He knew He could trust Dr. Mary Jones to do His will and to teach others how to trust Him. This is what she did.

She would not let people put their trust and confidences in her. She was happy to show them the way to trust the Almighty God. He who would do the same for them that, he did for her if they could only trust Him.

When some apostles, prophets, evangelist, pastors, and teachers were trying to pay off their churches with a thirty-year mortgage, God used this woman of God to pay off her first church in five months. To God be the glory.

Miracle of Faith: The Church Was Paid Off

As if that was not enough, God enabled the woman and man of God to purchase a second church. This one was located on the Eastside of town.

This church was not a storefront church, but it was a beautiful brick church that would be used to reach souls for the kingdom of God on the Eastside of town. Church services were held in both locations.

Again to God goes the glory and honor, for working miracles and building the faith of many.

Apostle Mary Jones dared to believe God and stand upon His word. The Word of God says for us to ask and it shall be given and to seek and ye shall find it. He says to knock and the doors shall be opened. Therefore, this woman asked and God gave her what she asked for and more.

When we say that God is able to provide exceeding and abundantly—above all we can ask or imagine—you can believe that He can. In this case, He did. We see again how God moved on behalf of His servant.

Half Million Dollar Church paid off in Seventeen Weeks

This time the gift was the biggest of all. God blessed the ministry with a three-story beautiful brick church and it is located on the North side of town.

We're for Jesus House of Prayer moved into a one thousand-seat sanctuary in 1986. The church and surrounding building were purchased for over $500,000. This too was paid off in less than six months!

Look what God will do when He can find a vessel to pour out His Spirit, power and anointing upon.

God begin to give the ministry more and more. There were houses on the boulevard that God gave for His glory and for His honor. There were houses in Amelia Island that members of the church and our guests could come, stay in, and enjoy for a very small fee.

Thank God for the ten-car garages and the long limo that God blessed the woman of God and her members.

There is a beautiful administration building that came with the purchase of the church. The church now has a multi-purpose building that was built in honor of the late Dr. Mary Austin Jones, and was named after her.

When we see God in His greatness, we realize that everything belongs to God. If we desire it, according to His word, we can have it.

The Bible says to ask and it shall be given. Seek and ye shall find. Knock and the doors shall be opened. The question is what do you want from God? Can you believe Him for it?

The ministry was truly blessed with so much more such as houses, vans, trucks, and cars. What a powerful and supernatural God we serve.

Apostle Dr. Mary Austin Jones was blessed to have outreach churches to serve under her. She was able to pray and watch for their souls as well.

She not only preaches the word in Jacksonville, but she was able to travel on foreign soil to preach the word of God.

This woman of God touches the heart of many men and women who needed healing in their bodies, deliverance for their souls, minds, and spirits.

Five Fold Ministry

Apostles, prophets, evangelists, pastors and teachers all seek the face of Jesus through this woman of God. They knew that God had appointed and called her for such a time as this.

I thank God today and always for such a vessel that has chosen to follow Him and to be there for those who He has called into ministry.

Ephesians 4:11 says:

And He gave some, apostles; and some prophets; and some evangelist; and some pastors and teachers;

For the perfecting of the saints, for the work of the ministry, for the edifying of the body of Christ:

That we henceforth be no more children, tossed to and fro, and carried about with every wind of doctrine, by the sleight of men, and cunning craftiness, whereby they lie in wait to deceive.

But speaking the truth in love may grow up into him in all things, which is the head, even Christ.

Why Some Preachers Are Not Fully Blessed

Some preachers of God could not be fully blessed because they gave glory to themselves instead of the Almighty God. They have forgotten that all the glory belongs to God.

Therefore, God could and did not use them the way He desired to use them. Some have been called but few have been chosen to carry out such an important mission.

Many people have gotten caught up in the flesh. They have been distracted with trying to please themselves instead of God. God was able to trust Dr. Mary Austin Jones with all of these things. She knew God would not allow her to take the glory for all that He has done in her life.

Many preachers of the gospel are like Nebuchadnezzar, the king in the book of Daniel, who in chapter 3 found himself wanting the people to worship him instead of God. Let's take a closer look at the king. He made an image of gold, whose height was threescore cubits and the breadth thereof six cubits. He set it up in the plain of Dura, in the province of Babylon.

Then Nebuchadnezzar the king sent to gather together the princes, governors, captains, judges, treasurers, counselors, sheriffs, and all the rulers of the provinces to come to the dedication of the image which Nebuchadnezzar himself had set up.

Then the princes, governors, captains, judges, treasurers, counselors, sheriffs, and all the rulers of the provinces were gathered together unto the dedication of the image that Nebuchadnezzar had set up.

Suddenly, a herald cried aloud,

To you it is commanded, O people, nations, and languages,

That at what time ye hear the sound of the cornet, flute, harp, sackbut, psaltery, dulcimer, and all kinds of music, ye fall down and worship the golden image that Nebuchadnezzar the king has set up:

And whoso falleth not down and worshipeth shall the same hour be cast into the midst of a burning fiery furnace.

When all the people heard the sound of the cornet, flute, harp, sackbut, psaltery, and all kinds of music, all the people, the nations, and languages, fell down and worshiped the golden image that Nebuchadnezzar the king had set up.

We are called to give all glory and honor to the King of Kings and the Lord of Lords. We are all servants of the Almighty God and God alone deserves to be so honored and praised.

Nebuchadnezzar put himself in the place of God and God had to bring judgment against him because he wanted the people to worship and praise him, instead of praising and worshiping God Almighty.

Yes, this woman of God brought Glory and honor to the Almighty God because there is no god before Him and there will be no god after Him.

Surgeon who Refused to Give God the Glory

Many years ago, I worked with a surgeon who did not fear God. There were times when he finished surgery and he would stand back and say that his surgery that he just completed looked better than what God created.

I often looked at him and thought, "What is wrong with this man? Why would he try and take the glory for something he did not do?"

I thank God for his mercy and grace because this surgeon could have suffered the same judgment that Nebuchadnezzar suffered. God could have allowed him to graze in the grass like this king until he acknowledged the Almighty God.

Education and wealth are wonderful, but there are people who forget that they could not learn or articulate if it is not granted by God.

Dr. Mary Austin Jones realized that the God she served and believed in was the same God who created the heavens and Earth. He was omnipresent because God is a Spirit. He is present everywhere all at once.

He is not limited to a particular place. When Solomon built the temple, he observed that no structure could contain the Lord, much less the beautiful temple that he would complete for God (2 Chronicle 6:18).

The psalmist David ask, whither shall I go from thy Spirit? Or whither shall I flee from thy presence; If I ascend up into heaven, thou art there: If I make my bed in hell, behold, thou art there Psalm 139:7, 8 (KJV).

David was assured that the Lord would guide and uphold him wherever he went.

I believe that our God gave the late Dr. Mary Austin Jones that same assurance that He would be with her.

She knew that her God was omniscient. He was not just limited by space, but unlimited in wisdom, knowledge, and understanding. When we look at God's servant Job, we see that he understood that it was God alone who gives us the understanding to solve life's problems.

Job held to his confidence in God, even when things did not seem to flow in his life. The Apostle Jones always sought the Lord Jesus Christ to solve problems in her life. God never did leave her or forsake her.

I am so glad that God alone is aware of all things. He knows the thoughts and actions of every person even before they ask. He does, we can put our total trust and confidence in Him.

The Apostle Paul says, "That wisdom and knowledge are unsearchable." It is beyond our ability to fully understand. This is why God is greater than us. Therefore, He deserves all of our praise.

Dr. Mary Austin Jones also knew that our God was omnipotent, which lets us know that He is all-powerful and that He can do all things. I do believe that this woman of God took God at His word and moved in faith and confidence in His word.

When God changed her life, she stayed before God in prayer and in thanksgiving. She did not put people or things first in her life, but she chose to forget about all the things that she had acquired. As a woman who was married to a police officer, who provided for her, her children, and she was thankful for all that her husband did. However, when she met Jesus, these things were no longer more important to her than her relationship with her God.

She did not let what she had in life stop her from ministering to God's people. She did not let her nice home, furniture, or anything else separate her from what God had called her to do. She allowed people to come into her home as she ministered the word of God.

She wrote on her living room wall these words, *Praise Ye the Lord of Host.* It was no longer about things. Instead it was all about God.

She was concerned for the souls of God's people; those who had not yet given their lives to him. I remember a tract that was written by her which was titled "Do You Know What Time It Is?"

Do You Know What Time It Is?

In it, she said, "You may look at the trees and flowers and tell what season it is. You may look at your watch and tell what hour of the day it is. You can even go to your calendar to see what month it is, but the Bible states in

Isaiah 63:4, 'The year of the redeemed is come.' Also, it is written, 'Now is the day of salvation.'" (11 Cor. 6:2)

The Lord will return soon and receive those who have accepted him in their heart; those who have been Born Again of the Spirit of God, the ones who live holy and sin not. If you are not numbered with the holy ones today, the Spirit of the Lord says to you to "Repent", for the kingdom of Heaven is at hand. Commit sin no more.

Do you know what time it is that the Lord is coming? It is that the Lord is coming back like a thief in the night, but of the day and hour knoweth no man. No, not the angels of heaven, but my Father only. But as the days of Noah were, so shall the coming of the Son of man be. For as in the days that were before the flood, they were eating, drinking, marrying and giving in marriage, until the day Noah entered into the ark and knew not until the flood came and took them all away. So shall the coming of the Son of man be. (St. Matthew 24:36-39)

Don't risks you're life on a Season of good times, die, and go to Hell. That is where you're going if you haven't made Jesus your Choice.

He says in Revelation 3:17:

Because thou sayest I am rich, and increased with goods, and have need of nothing; and knoweth not that thou are wretched, and miserable and poor, and blind, and naked. You may say why does he say these things? The answer is simple- — you don't have Him living and abiding on the inside. Inside of what you ask-your heart. Yes, your heart. The Lord says, "Behold I stand

*at the door and knock; if any man hears My voice and open the
door. I will come unto him.*

(Revelation 3:20)

Do you know what time it is? It's time to serve God. It's
time to let people see Christ in you by living holy, faithful,
and righteous lives unto God. You'll have a better time
serving God than serving sin.

The Painted Sepulchers

By Apostle Dr. Mary Austin Jones

June, 1996, she wrote the Painted Sepulchers. I would like
to share her writing with you.

"In the day that you hear my voice, harden not your
heart." We do serve a God who is able to speak to His
People. Today, He is speaking to His People; those who
are called by His Name. He does not want you beautifying
the outside when you're inside (your heart) are filthy. It's
time for you to hear what God has to say to the church
(you, not a building made of bricks and mortar). The woe
has gone out because God wants His people to bring
glory to His name.

There are not many passages of scripture that talk about
being painted. However, I would like to call your attention
to St. Matthew, Chapters 23:25-29.

Woe unto you scribes and Pharisees, hypocrites! For ye make clean the outside of the cup and of the platter but within they are full of extortion and excess. Thou, blind Pharisee, clean first that which is within the cup and platter that the outside of them may be clean also. Woe unto you Scribe and Pharisee, Hypocrites! For ye are like unto whited sepulchers, which indeed appear beautiful outward, but are within full of dead men's bones, and of all uncleanness. Even so, ye also outwardly appear righteous unto men, but within ye are full of hypocrisy and iniquity. Woe unto you, Scribes and Pharisees, hypocrites! Because ye build the tomb of the prophets, and garnish the sepulchers of the righteous.

God is calling you to be leader, examples, and witnesses, but more than anything, He wants you to be real. He does not want you to be like the Pharisee and Scribes. He does not want you painted on the outside and unclean on the inside. He does not want you to pretend to be something that you're not. You must pray like the Psalmist David prayed when he said, "Lord created in me a clean heart and renewed a right spirit within me."

Many of you are trying to paint a picture of being something that you're not. What's your motive for trying to beautify the outside? Who are you trying to impress? Are you trying to bring attention to yourself or to God?

We are seeing too many people with titles in the Body of Christ that fail to exemplify the power of the Holy Ghost. The church (which consists of you, not a building) is to be an example to the world. The church is trying to change to be like the world and this should not be. Why, because you are the salt of the earth! The world should be trying to be like the church! It's time to take a look at yourself and let God know that you want to change. We have too many choir members, preachers, and ushers painted. Meanwhile, God is saying, *"let's get the inside clean."*

Let me tell you. When you say you want to please God, there are some sacrifices that that must be made. All of those personality traits that don't line up with the Word of God it must be destroyed. Why, because old things pass away and behold; all things become new.

We are already made, but God is saying there is something about the inside of us that's not right. We need to acknowledge that we need help. Once we do, God will begin to rearrange and fix us up. He will remove some things and remake us in His image. It's time for us to re-establish ourselves.

Come Out Of Poverty

Dr. Mary Austin Jones's message to the people of God

Beloved, I wish above all things that thou mayest prosper and be in health even as thy soul prospereth. God is concerned about the whole man. In order for you to proper, you first must have your soul prospering.3rd John

Some people may tell you that if you have a raggedy car, you should not ask God for a brand new one. The God I serve is rich in houses and land. I found out through the word of God that I did not need to settle for anything. I want to share this with you. You do not have to settle for anything.

There are many church-going people who say they know God who is still suffering, still dying of sickness, sin, diseases, and still living in poverty.

We're going to come out of this poverty!!! God said to preach the gospel to the poor. He did not say this, so they could stay poor. God wants you to know that the poor needs help and our help cometh from the Lord; who made the heaven and the Earth.

I want to remind you not to be caught up in finances because of the second verse of III John. God is concerned about your physical and spiritual health as well as your financial well being.

All of that damnable doctrine you have heard in times past, telling you that God does not want you to have different things; to just be satisfied with what you have— forget it!

The Lord lets us know in His word that we are to seek first His kingdom and His righteousness (not the material wealth of this world) and these other things that you've desired shall be added unto you.

You see, I was not down on my knees saying, "Give me, give me; God, I need furs and I need diamonds". These things couldn't save me, they couldn't heal me, they couldn't comfort me, and they couldn't do what I needed to have done in my life.

When God saved me, He became #1 in my life. He made the difference in me! I delight myself in the Lord and He rewards me by giving me the desires of my heart.

His words tell us to delight thyself in the Lord and He shall give thee the desires of thine heart. "God is not a man that He should lie. If He said it, He is able to perform it!

COME OUT OF POVERTY!!!

It's time for us to be what God has made us to be. It's time for us to walk in the place of prosperity—spiritually, physically, and financially.

It is written in Proverbs 10:22: "The blessing of the Lord maketh rich and He addeth no sorrow with it."

Either you're blessed or you're cursed. Whom God blesseth, no witch, no root worker, no sorcerer—they can't curse you.

No weapon that would be formed against you will prosper. WE'RE **COMING OUT OF POVERTY!!!**

The 28th chapter of Deuteronomy backs up everything I've said thus far.

Some of you think the only way you can make it is out in the world is by serving the devil. I want you to know that God has plan that surpasses that of the crack dealer.

If you shall hearken diligently to the voice of the Lord, thy God, to observe and to do all His commandments, the Lord, thy God, will set thee on high above all nations of the Earth. All these blessings shall come on thee and overtake thee.

Blessed shall you be in the city and blessed you be in the field.

Blessed shall be the fruit of thy body and the fruit of thy ground (you can see God is concerned about your children too). And the fruit of thou cattle, the increase of thine kine and flock of thy sheep. Blessed shall thou be when thou comest in and blessed shall thou be when thou goest out. The Lord shall cause thine enemies (you who?) that rise up against thee to be smitten (in other words defeated), before thy face, (not behind your back, you'll be able to see it for yourself). They shall come out against thee one way and flee before the seven ways (they will recognize that God is with you).

The Lord shall open unto Thee His Good Treasures

The Lord shall command the blessings upon thee and thy storehouse, and all that thou settest thine hand unto and He shall bless thee in the land which the Lord giveth thee. The Lord, (not your pastor), shall establish thee and holy people unto himself. As He has sworn onto thee if thou shall keep the commandments of the Lord thy God and walk in His way and all people of the earth shall see that thou are called by the name of the Lord and they shall be afraid of thee and the Lord, (not the devil, not your employer), shall thee plenteous in goods in the fruit of thy body and in the fruit of thy cattle and in the fruit of thy ground and the land which the Lord sware unto they father to give thee.

The Lord shall open unto thee His good treasures. The heaven to give the rain unto thy land in its season and to bless all the work of thy hands, (anything you put your hands unto—you your families delivered).

You want a better place to live? You want a promotion? You want to drive a nice car? He said everything you put your hands unto shall be blessed, you shall lend unto many nations and thou shall not borrow.

The Lord shall make thee the head and not the tail. Thou shall be above only and thou shall not be beneath. If thou hearken unto the commandments of the Lord, thy God, which I command thee this day to observe and to do them, and thou shall not go astray from any of the words which I command thee this day—to the right hand or to the left—to go after other gods to serve them. Remember—the blessing of the Lord maketh rich. Somebody ought to say; LORD, MAKE ME RICH!

Apostle Dr. Mary Austin Jones Stood the Test of Time *in Ministry*

Today, as you read the words of the Designer Originals, you can see a woman of God whose fruits yet remain. This is because she chose to serve the true and living God.

She served Him with all of her heart, mind, soul, and spirit. Apostle Dr. Mary Austin Jones is one of those women who stood the test of time. She is now an example for those who can take God at His word. I thank my God for my formal Overseer and founder of the *We're For Jesus House of Prayer.* I am thankful that God allowed me to spend 27 years with her, at a church where God used the woman of God to do great and mighty things in the name of the Jesus. It was there that the woman of God heard His voice. She ordained me, several other men, and women of God as Assistant Pastors to preach the word in and out of season.

They included Pastor Yvette Williams, Pastor Elijah Johnson, Pastor Todney Bynes, Pastor Mary Smith McCoy, Pastor Tyrinda Dixon, Pastor Gaylinda Henderson, and Pastor Arthur Jackson

We all were ordained as her Assistant Pastors for the work of the ministry.

The day that my Overseer passed on from this life to be with our Lord, all of us were at one place or another. I was at work in surgery when my supervisor came in to let me know that my pastor had passed away. As I remember that day, my eyes are full of tears because of what she meant to me and to the people of God. I know now why God has trusted me to write about such a beautiful woman of God; one who was so bold in every way.

The night she went to be with Lord was a Friday night. It happened to be my time to preach and minister the word to God's people.

I had to preach as though our Overseer was present because that was the way that she would have wanted me to preach. She once spoke to the church after I had witness to the Ku Klux Klan's. She was so proud of me and she told the church that I reminded her of David in the word of God.

At that time, it was on every channel in our city and because of her stand on certain issues she made mention of what God had done.

Although all of us were hurting, we all had to remain strong for the people of God so that they could hear the word of God and be encouraged.

God's Designer Original

On February 25, 2005, God, Designer Original—the woman who stood the test of time and who stood on the front lines in her love, commitment, and faith to the Almighty God and her Lord and Savior, Jesus Christ. She departed this life on Earth to spend forever in her new home. She went to see our heavenly father, His angels, and those who have gone before her. She went to take her place in the kingdom that God has prepared for his precious daughter.

Apostle Dr. Jeannette C. Holmes-Vann

Dr. Jeannette Holmes-Vann is another icon and a woman that God created to stand on the front lines. This woman is extremely bold and courageous. She is a woman God has chosen to reach a mass of people for the kingdom of God. Her faith in God has allowed her to stand in a day and time when it was not popular to be a woman in ministry. She was not moved by what people said or did. She was determined to do the will of the Father.

She was the first child of Harvey Cofer and Gladys Gibbs.

Her mother decided to relocate the family to Bayard, Florida, which was located in a rural suburb of Jacksonville.

Dr. Holmes-Vann helped to provide the care for her eight younger brothers and sisters while her mother worked outside of the home. Dr. Holmes-Vann was like a mother to her sisters and brothers. She provided for them in a way that only God could have taught her.

As the oldest child, she was given the responsibility of taking care of her siblings. She was expected to take care of them like her mother would take care of them, if she had been home with them.

At times, she enforced corrections when necessary. However, more often she would take the time to listen to them or just smile or laugh with her siblings as their caretaker.

The Making of a True Leader

Dr. Holmes-Vann has always reminded me of David, who God trusted to take care of His father's sheep. David loved the sheep and he protected them at all costs. I remember when the lion and the bear approached the sheep. David fought them to make sure that the sheep were protected, because the sheep could not protect themselves.

When I think of this young woman who was given the responsibility to take care of her siblings, I realize this was God's way of preparing her to take care of His sheep as a pastor.

The woman of God was also taking care of the house while her mother went out to support the family. In this way, she was able to meet the needs of the family by cooking, and washing the clothes, and making sure that she did all the things her mother would have done. When I think of Apostle Holmes-Vann, I think of the grooming that God will do in our lives, preparing us for our futures.

It took time, effort, and commitment to do the job expected of her. Likewise, it takes time for us to do what God has call us to do. How could this woman of God have been obedient to God if she had not first been obedient to her mother? We thank God that she was obedient to her mother and the Almighty God.

She had to give an answer to her mother, if she did not take care of the house and children. She had to give an account of what was done and what was not done while her mother was at work.

This is the way that the people of God will give an account of what we say or do. God was preparing her to take care of His sheep. Also, I believe God was showing her how to love her siblings and care for them because one day she would have to do the same for God's people.

She had to learn how to lead, guide, and direct them along their paths, so that they would not be unwise in their decision-making. This was so they could be good examples to their children and to others.

Dr. Holmes-Vann is a great example of a true leader. A leader is one that others will follow. They are people blessed with a clear vision and purpose.

Miles Monroe said, "That leaders are not born; they are made!" Dr. Holmes-Vann was made a leader by God. When she was in her mother's womb, God had a plan for her life. He knew that this woman of God would be one of His leaders. She would lead, guide, and direct His people in the way that they should go.

She would be one of his leaders, created to take God at His word. She would not hesitate to go forward in the things of God.

When Moses was in his mother's womb, God had already ordained him to be a leader. He made sure that when the Pharaoh decided to kill all the baby boys, this baby would not be destroyed.

God's plan for him was to lead His people out of Egypt. God knew that there were many of His people that did not want to be stranded without knowing and experiencing a new life in Christ. He wanted them to benefit from the true revelation and knowledge of our Lord and Savior Jesus Christ.

Why should God's people settle for just anything when God is everything we need?

We need to stop living beneath our privilege. When I think about Dr. Holmes-Vann, she did not struggle with what God asked her to do. She just did it.

When she heard His voice, she did not harden her heart toward God. She was obedient to the call of God. The instructions given to her were clear. All she was expected to do was to obey. Why would it ever be difficult for people who say they love God to follow His Instructions?

Tradition and Legalism

When God called on Moses, He called him to deliver those who were captive and imprisoned. Similarly, God called on Apostle Holmes-Vann to bring many people out of tradition and legalism, so that they could be free to hear and follow Him. God wants His people to have sustaining power to live according to the word of God.

Sometimes people are afraid to answer the call. They refuse to allow God to use them and even put them on the pottery wheel. This way God can take away that old man who is sometimes still a part of their lives and change them into a beautiful vessel for His glory and honor.

When they do not allow God to keep working on them; the gospel and winning souls will never rise to a place where God can truly use them.

Can God Trust You with His Ministry

When God called Moses, it was clear that Moses was not perfect. The same was true in the life of Dr. Jeanette C Holmes-Vann. He knew He could trust her with a ministry and with His people.

When Moses was called by God, he was afraid. He did not know what to do or say to the people or to the Pharaoh. But God showed him everything he needed to know. It is in this same way that God showed Dr. Holmes-Vann what to do.

Every idea she had—ideas which made her ministry so successful—came directly from God Almighty.

The day she went back home from church and went before God was the beginning of her walk with Christ Jesus.

Men and woman of God must first repent before the Almighty God, humble themselves, so that God can use them to bring them into fellowship with Him.

When we read the book 2 Chronicle 7:14, it says, "If my people, who are called by My name, shall humble themselves, pray, seek My face, and turn from their wicked ways; then will I hear from heaven, I will forgive their sin, and will heal their land."

God has allowed her to walk in this office of the five-fold ministry, she had to be useful to God to bring correction to the body of Christ; so that they will live and not die.

Church has always been a part of Dr. Holmes-Vann's life. Her mother insisted on regular church attendance.

I would like to give honor to a woman who I have never had the privilege of meeting. However, Dr. Holmes-Vann's mother was one of those special women who wanted the best for her daughter and children. Her mother knew how important it was to have a relationship with Jesus Christ and to have a good education.

I believe she received a basic foundation from the church she attended, but she never experienced knowing Jesus Christ as her personal Savior. Therefore, she did not know Him and her life in Christ was incomplete.

Devine Connections

How can we live for Christ when we do not know Christ and when we have not been Born Again? I believe that this was God at work in the life of the Apostle.

In her adult years, Dr. Holmes-Vann grew increasingly dissatisfied with her life and the the church as she knew it. Her heart's desire grew, and she declared, "Lord, I want to help."

There are so many people who go to church each Sunday who lack a personal relationship with the God who made and created them. This was the case for Apostle Holmes-Vann.

They are people who attend church because their parents and friends are going. They attend church, but their lives have not been changed.

They are hearing the preacher preach the word, but their heart has not been changed. I feel regret when I think about the millions of people who are taking the time to get out of their warm beds, get dressed, and prepare to go into the house of the Lord every Sunday without the word of God ever penetrating the innermost parts of their mind, soul, and spirit.

They go in to hear the word, but how many of them are submitting to the call of Jesus Christ in their hearts. Many people think if they go to church that is all they need to do; that is just the beginning. You can take the natural bread in your hand, but if you do not take a bite and chew on it; you will never receive the benefits of the bread.

This is the same in the word of God. If we fail only to handle and touch the outside of the Holy Bible, it will do us no good. We need to read it and digest the bible. When we do this we can acquire a taste for the bread that will give us that everlasting life.

It is clear that Dr. Jeanette C. Holmes-Vann was brought up in a church, but the church was not in her. When the word of God comes into our lives; we become a walking and living Church of God.

She realized that going to church was good, but that it could not fill the innermost parts of her mind, body, soul, and spirit. She needed someone who had truly digested the word of God and had become a living testimony and witness of the true and living God.

Anything that is not alive needs to be buried. The blind cannot lead the blind into eternity life in Christ.

Spiritual Encounter

Even though she had been involved in the church all her life, she had not yet met "the God of the church." As the fullness of time approached, a humble and unassuming deacon at her local church (Jerusalem Baptist Church) named Joseph Thomas—a man with no more than a 3rd grade education—began to cry loud and spare not.

"If you don't know that you know you are saved . . ." he began.

These words disturbed Dr. Holmes-Vann deep within her spirit. Just before the church service began, Dr. Holmes—Vann recalled that she heard in her spirit the voice of the Lord telling her to "go home."

In obedience to this emphatic command, she headed for home on the north side of Jacksonville in the Sherwood Forest community. When she arrived, the same voice spoke again as she approached her front door.

"Come on in," it said.

Once inside, again the voice of the Lord spoke.

"Come on down."

Dr. Holmes-Vann hastened downstairs to her basement. There, as she knelt upon a large burnt-orange pillow, she completely surrendered herself to the Lord. She remembers that after her encounter with the Lord, once again the voice of God spoke.

"Get up," the voice said. "You're alright now."

God, through His grace, and her faith in Jesus Christ, saved her. A few days later, God miraculously baptized her in His Holy Spirit, thus preparing her to be a witness of the miraculous saving power of Jesus Christ.

First Prayer Meeting

Immediately after the life changing experience with God, the First prayer meeting took place on Tuesday night in her basement. Sister Holmes, as she was known at the time, had given her life to Christ. There were four people in attendance. The woman of God never opened the Bible that night. She simply told with great conviction what had happened to her, how she found what she was looking for, and what she desperately needed.

She continued to hold Tuesday night meetings, where those present would pray, listen to gospel albums, sing familiar Gospel hymns, share their testimonies, and share in the word of God.

They were times of great excitement for the newness and reality of God's presence. Anointing continued to fill their heart with anticipation and zeal. Those who were there compared these times to the Azusa Street revival.

As the Lord continued to add souls to the kingdom, they decided upon a name for their group. The group was call Unity, Prayer, Bible And Mission Outreach. Prayer and Bible study began to be held in Sister Holmes's newly added garage. It was complete with a piano and an aisle down the middle. In spite of the cramped conditions, nothing seemed capable of stopping the people from coming. If there were no seats available inside, people would simply stand outside. If it were raining, people would stand under umbrellas.

Florida's summer heat did not deter the saints, even though it appeared at times that the walls and ceiling were sweating from the humidity. Not even the mosquitoes could keep the sincere from receiving the Word. A large speaker was set up outside for those who couldn't get inside. Those who were saved would offer their seats inside to visitors, so that they could hear the life-changing word of God more comfortably.

Communion and foot washing services would be held in the backyard to accommodate everyone. Curious neighbors would stand across the fence and watch the service from afar. On some Friday nights, there would even be shuts-ins with fervent prayer occurring throughout the night.

As the meetings continued, the meeting place began to alternate between the north and southside of Jacksonville. Tuesday night services were held in the garage on Roanoke, while Thursday night services were held on the southside of town in the garage of Sister Ethel Bryant.

Seeking God Direction for Church Building

In 1977, the Apostle Holmes-Vann asked God where she and the others could find a home for their church. Due to her dissatisfaction with denominational church and the drawback in her spirit, Sunday mornings would usually be spent at home reading her Bible. She had not been led to go to any church in particular.

God simply told her, "be still, just be still."

For a long time, no offering was taken. Pastor Holmes-Vann freely gave up her home for the work of the ministry, absorbing all the cost by herself. Later now it became necessary for God to lead Pastor Holmes-Vann to receive offerings from group members. God gave her the understanding that giving was a necessary part of Christian development. This was the way of providing blessings to the saints. Taking nothing for herself, she would take the offerings and put it in the bank, waiting for God to show her how to use it.

Miracle of Faith: 51 Acres of Land!

Eventually, it became apparent that Hope Chapel would have to find a permanent home. God miraculously provided. Just around the corner from the Pastor's home on Roanoke Blvd., sat 51 acres of untouched land just waiting to be discovered. The landowner, Roy Crumbly, who remains a friend of the ministry to this day, was contacted and offers were made. With the touch of God, Pastor Holmes-Vann was able to purchase 2.5 acres of land with cash.

The first edifice would be called the fellowship, because Pastor Holmes-Vann knew that this was the beginning of what God was doing. She knew that soon there would be a need for a much larger building for the saints to gather. Sanctuary was already in her vision.

In 1988, God spoke to her again. It was time for her vision to take another step forward. The pastor spoke it into the atmosphere—it is time to make preparations to build our Main Sanctuary!

That which had been spoken from God from eternity, into the heart of the Pastor, was made manifest in the earthly realm.

Dedication of Hope Chapel New Church

Almost ten years to the day after the dedication of the fellowship hall, it was time to dedicate their Main Sanctuary!

The year 1993, brought more construction to the Hope Chapel campus, with the renovation, and dedication of the original Fellowship Hall. It was time to expand, as with all things, and it was done in grand style.

The Fellowship Hall grew to three times its original size. It became the location for their Bible Studies, Prayer service, plays, even banquets, and weekly dining.

A great fire came in 1996, but this was not a destructive fire; it was a liberating fire. After five short years of occupying their new Sanctuary, Hope Chapel burned its 30-year mortgage and was again debt-free. The chapel would never go in debt again, and hasn't to this day.

By this time, it was time to build a school. But as they would find out, their vision was much smaller than the one God had placed in the heart of their Pastor.

Apostle Jeanette C. Holmes-Vann eventually became the Founder and Superintendent of Esprit de Corps Center for Learning once it was constructed. As the Queen of Shea said to Solomon, only the half has been told.

Hope Chapel Christian Fellowship has done great and mighty things through the leadership and direction of God, the Holy Spirit. There have been several more buildings constructed on the campus of this great church. I believe that there will be more to come as well.

Biblical Women Who Stood the Test of Time

There are many women in the bible that stood on the front lines of time. These are women who God used to make a difference from one generation to the next. They refused to be silent and compromise the perfect will of God in their lives.

When we think about women such as Hannah, it is easy to see that she was faithful in her prayers to God.

When we look at 1 Samuel 1:1 through 2:10, we see that she was the mother of the prophet, Samuel, who was the last judge of Israel.

Hannah was barren and without a child for many years. She prayed to God to answer her prayers and it seemed as though God didn't hear her. However, this did not keep her from praying and crying out to God to hear her prayers.

God was well aware of her plight and longing to embrace a child, but our time is not always God's time. When we read the word of God, we see that our God did move on her behalf. She had to wait on God and be courageous. As women of God, we must always pray and not faint from challenges. We must always be steadfast, unmovable in our faith, and commitment to our Creator.

As women of God, there are events in our lives that lead us to surrender more and more to His will and power. I believe that this is a good thing, so that God can use us in a more perfect way.

Hannah grew more persistent in her prayer to the Almighty God because of her strong desire to have this child.

God was creating in her a greater desire for this child. She couldn't have known that she was going to give birth to a Judge and prophet of God.

Although she was suffering and being ridiculed by Peninnah, she stood fast in her faith in God.

When we see Hannah, we see a woman who was faithful in her prayer to God, even when her adversary came up against her, to provoke her, to make her fret, because the Lord had closed her womb.

Hannah felt bitterness in her soul, and prayed unto the Lord and wept.

She made a vow, saying, "Oh, Lord of hosts, if thou wilt indeed look on the affliction of thine handmaid, remember me, and not forget thine handmaid, but wilt give unto thine handmaid a man child. Then, I will give unto the Lord all the days of his life, and there shall no razor come upon his head."

As women of God, it seems like we are often in a battle all by ourselves. We must always remember that the battle does not belong to us, but to God. This is not our battle. This is not our fight, but it all belongs to God.

Hannah wanted this child so much that she was willing to give him back to God. It there anything that is in our lives that we will be willing to give it back to God, so that He can use it for His glory and for His honor.

Hannah could not see this at first because she was all about her wants and desires. When it became about God, He granted her petition unto her.

Women of God, your desires may not be for a son or daughter. It could be for a closer walk with our Lord. Don't give up and don't give in. Allow God to mature our faith and confidence in Him, so that you can have that same faith and love for God that she had in Him, to be able to trust God completely.

Yes, these are great and committed women of the Bible who are willing to show you how to believe God in every area of our lives.

The reference is 1 Samuels, 1:1 through 2:10

Can you believe God for every small, great thing in your lives? In the end, it does matter. Christ wants us to believe that He can do it. We begin today? We can pray and believe God for anything in our lives, such as salvation, deliverance, a job, an education, a home, healing, mercy, faith, loneness, forgiveness, and anything that we need from day to day? To do so, we must be willing to wait on God for every request or petition.

If Hannah could wait, so can we.

Ruth Restores Hope

Reference: Ruth 1:1 through 4:22

Ruth is another great woman of God that I would like to bring back to your remembrance. God uses her to help restore hope to those who remain faithful to Him.

There are many people in our world who have lost hope. It could be in their job, a friend, a husband or whatever the situation may be. We need to keep our eyes on the only one who is faithful righteous, and one who we can rely on every day of the week. I know seven days a week, twenty-four hours of the day, we can depend on God.

When we lose faith, hope, and confidence in Christ, it is possible that life can become unbearable.

It is said that a prisoner without hope may break down long before his date of release.

A patient without hope deteriorates and often dies. When we study the book of Ruth, we see how God brought a family through a season of hopelessness that had a great effect upon their lives.

There have been times when we have seen the homeless on the street, and we may have given them a few dollars for their needs. This helps us us feel that we have helped someone in their time of need. What happens when you find yourself in the same situation that the homeless person was facing?

Ruth and her family found themselves in a desperate place of need. She had lost her husband, leaving her a widow in a foreign land.

Her mother-in-law, Naomi, had lost her sons and husband and it seemed like there was no hope for them. They had almost given up on life, because they could not see the end of the hardness and pain they were enduring. This is much like it often is in the hearts of men and women today, but our faith is not in man or in what we see; it is in God.

Ruth said to Naomi, "that she would not leave thee, or return from following after thee."

For whither thou goest, I will go; and where thou lodgest, I will lodge: thy people shall be my people, and thy God my God:

Where thou diest, will I die, and there will I buried: the Lord do so to me more also, if aught but death part thee and me.

The book of Ruth begins with the famine in the land, in those days the Judges ruled.

Elimelech went to Moab with his wife, Naomi, and his sons, Mahlon and Chilion. It had to be a distressing time to see that an Israelite family would leave the Promised Land. This reveals the distressing times they were living in.

The word reveals to us that Elimelech soon died and both of their son's married Moabite women; a practice that was discouraged by the law. Later we read that both of Naomi's sons also died.

Naomi decided she was going to return home, but she did not expect her two daughter's in-law to return with her.

We see Orpah in tearful farewell, but Ruth had a strong love for Naomi. Therefore, she clung to Naomi, because her relationship was not just with a relative, but with a woman who was seeking God.

Ruth found something in Naomi that she did not want to depart. It was then that they returned to Judah. When we can see Jesus in another individual, we can see hope. I believe it was her day-to-day lifestyle that made Ruth sees not just another mother-in-law, but someone who made her want to leave her own people and follow a woman who could not give Ruth another husband. In the end, what God had in mind for both of them was incredible.

Hebrews 11:1

Faith is the substance of all things hoped for. It is the evidence of things not seen.

Ruth may not have been able to have a husband or child from another of Naomi's sons, but she had faith to believe in the God she served. The God that Naomi served led her back to a place where she and her daughter knew they would be taken care of; where there was no famine and better days lay ahead. Difficult days were behind them.

When we can be women on the front lines of time, we can cause others to live and prosper in the things of God.

Orpah had a vision, but it was not the same vision as Ruth's. She knew that her husband was dead and she was not willing to stay in a place where there seemed to be no hope.

When we see Jesus, we can see protection, provision, and resources. Orpha could not see any of these things. Therefore, she decided to leave her mother-in-law and her sister-in-law, to return home to a people who did not believe or worship God.

We are so blessed to have had an encouraging encounter with Jesus Christ. This leads us to know the will of the father, which is so encouraging to me. We know we can stand on the word of God and trust Him to take care of every problem and concern in our lives.

Yes, we are women of faith and our faith is in God. We know that God has touched our lives and made us unafraid to take our stand on issues of survival for millions of people. No, we are not the same individuals we were before we met Jesus.

He has taught us how to trust and depend upon Him. Even in desperate times we know we can count on Him.

When there is no money in the bank, we can count on him. When there is no gas in the car, we can count on Him. Even when there seems to be no job on the horizon, we know we can count on him.

Psalms 37: 25-26

I have been young, and now I am old; yet have I not seen the righteous forsaken, nor his seed begging bread.

He is ever merciful, and lendeth; and his seed is blessed.

Can a Ninety Year old Woman Give Birth to a Child?

Genesis 17:16; 15-21

I will bless her, and give thee a son also of her: yea, I will bless her, and she shall be a mother of nations; kings of people shall be of her.

Then Abraham fell upon his face, and laughed, and said in his heart, Shall a child be born unto him that is a hundred years old? And shall Sarah, that is ninety years old, bear?

And Abraham said unto God, O that Ishmael might live before thee!

And God said Sarah thy wife shall bear thee a son indeed; and thou shalt call his name Isaac: and I will establish my covenant with him for an everlasting covenant and with his seed after him.

There are women on the front lines of time that God has chosen to use. They were chosen when they were old and seemed like they were ready for a rocking chair, but God wants the world to see Jesus in the elderly as well. God is still doing great and mighty things in every human being, if they just can believe Him, even when things look impossible.

I was told of a woman who was getting up at the age of 101 and helping to comb others' hair. This is the same woman who was shopping and living on her own.

Can God use these same women to heal the sick and raise the dead? Yes, He can. Can He use these same women to preach the gospel and feed the homeless? Yes, He can.

Sarah Conceived In Her Old Age Isaac

Genesis 21:1

And the Lord visited Sarah as He had said, and the Lord did unto Sarah as He had spoken.

For Sarah conceived, and bore Abraham a son in his old age, at the set time of which God had spoken to him.

And Abraham called the name of his son that was born unto him, whom Sarah bore to him, Isaac.

Genesis 21:6-7

And Sarah said:

God hath made me to laugh, so that all here will laugh with me.

And she said, who would have said unto Abraham, that Sarah should have given children suck? For I have borne him a son in his old age.

God will always keep His promises! And even as God kept His promise to Abraham He will keep His word to us.

We can no longer put our talents, purpose, gifts, and calling on the back line, we must allow God to use us for His glory and for His honor.

Sarah did not realize that she once again could laugh about something that seemed too hard for women of her age. She could be married to a man who was 100 years old and she was 90 years old.

If we can only believe God, He will show you greater things. These miracles will allow you to build the faith of many and cause the unbelievers to be saved and made free.

For the word of God said whom the Son has made free is free indeed.

Don't Give Up!

There are many times Christians become weary in their quest to wait on God to fulfill all of the promises He has for them.

There are times when they think that God will not answer their prayers. When we see these two individuals, we can be sure that God will keep His promises.

We need to submit ourselves to God and respond when He asks something of our time, faith, and commitment to Him.

When we refuse to obey God, we can hinder God's plans for our lives. When we obey and He is pleased with us, He can use us for His glory.

It is time for every man, woman, boy, and girl to allow the Holy Spirit to lead; guide and direct their path so that we can all see more of the Supernatural blessing of God. In this way we can see that the signs of the believer will follow every believer in the Holy Ghost.

Signs of a True Believer

Mark 16: 15

And he said unto them, Go ye into all the world, and preach the gospel to every creature.

He that believeth and is baptized shall be saved; but he that believeth not shall be damned.

And these signs shall follow them that believe; In my name shall they cast out devils; they shall speak with new tongues;

They shall take up serpents; and if they drink any deadly thing, it shall not hurt them; they shall lay hand on the sick, and they shall recover.

Sleeping Giants in the Church Please Wake up!

I pray that this book has been a blessing and a stepping stone for every believer. My desire is only to bring glory to God and to wake up the sleeping giants that live within the body of Christ.

God has created these women to stand on the front lines of our times. They have served as true examples for the body of Christ.

I honor God for all the men and women of God who stand and lift up His name. These are people who refuse to be lukewarm and stagnant in their walk with Christ.

If we are going to do anything for the cause of Christ, *now is the time*. Too many people are on their way to hell. Where are the people who are crying loudly and sparing not? Where are the people who are lifting up their voices like a trumpet, preaching, and teaching against their transgressions?

God loves them and yes, His desire is that they will be saved. Therefore, let us be examples of Christ like these women of God. Are they perfect? No, but God is, and He has chosen them to stand on the front lines of our times for Him.

Apostle Dr. Mary Austin Jones operated in the five-fold ministry gifts, as an apostle, pastor, prophet, evangelist, and teacher. She was a prayerful and financial supporter of foreign and local ministries, including a foreign radio station, and orphanage in Brazil. She was a firm believer in the word of God as it is written in Roman 13:8 and Matthew 25:21 respectively, "Owe no man anything, but to love one another . . ." and . . . "I will make thee ruler over many things."

Apostle Jones was a 1964 graduate of Matthew Gilbert High School. Also, she studied at Florida Community College of Jacksonville and Oral Roberts University. In 1988, she received an Honorary Doctorate of Sacred Scripture from United Christian College in New York.

Apostle Jones outreach ministry has taken her to Africa, Alaska, Germany, Turkey, Canada, Hawaii, Holland, Israel, and Russia. In addition, she traveled to numerous parts of Alabama, California, the Carolinas, Florida, Georgia, Louisiana, New York, Tennessee, and Washington.

While visiting The Holy Land (Israel), Apostle was afforded the opportunity to baptize and polish Christian believers in the famous Jordan River. As well as, preached on the Sea of Galilee in a large boat.

Apostle Dr. Jeannette C. Holmes-Vann was born in Macon, Georgia, the eldest of nine children. At an early age her family relocated to Jacksonville, Florida, where she attended the Duval County Public Schools.

Dr. Holmes—Vann is the wife of Brother Joe Louis Vann, the mother of three daughters (De Dra, Alison and & Kendrie), one son, Brandon and the proud grandmother of six.

Dr. Holmes-Vann's leadership ability and gift of administration is evident in the fact that she has overseen the building of every project of her multimillion—dollar ministry.

Primary, the ministry is dedicated to building and mending the lives of men and women, while helping to develop children into quality, productive adults. The ministry is also involved in outreach to the elderly, the incarcerated and those that are bound by sin and hopelessness. She has traveled extensively and ministered in various arenas. She is a trailblazer as well as an inspiration to many through her television and radio broadcast.

In her pursuit to serve God in holiness and excellence, her gifts of encouragement, organization and administration have caused noted evidence of excellence through—out the body of Christ.

Apostle Holmes—Vann has always been interested in learning as well as sharing her knowledge with others. For this reason, after graduating from High School, she continued her education at Edward Waters College, receiving Associate's and Bachelor's Degree in Physical Education, Health, and Science. She was then accepted into graduate school at Florida Agricultural and Mechanical University (FAMU) and obtained a Master's Degree in Education.